SPANISH MISSIONS

A TRUE BOOK®

by
Christin Ditchfield

Children's Press®
A Division of Scholastic Inc.

New York Toronto London Auckland Sydney
Mexico City New Delhi Hong Kong
Danbury, Connecticut

A statue
of Father
Junípero
Serra, who
founded
missions in
California

Content Consultant
Robert M. Senkewicz
*Professor of History, Santa
Clara University*

Reading Consultant
Dr. Cecilia Minden-Cupp
*Former Director, Language and
Literacy Program
Harvard Graduate School of
Education*

*The photograph on the cover
shows Mission San Carlos
Borromeo in Carmel, California.
The photograph on the title
page shows a bell tower at
Mission San Juan Bautista
in California.*

Library of Congress Cataloging-in-Publication Data
Ditchfield, Christin.
    Spanish missions / by Christin Ditchfield.
        p. cm. — (A true book)
    Includes bibliographical references and index.
    ISBN 0-516-22834-X (lib. bdg.)   0-516-21746-1 (pbk.)
    1. Franciscans—Missions—California—History—Juvenile literature.
2. Missions, Spanish—California—History—Juvenile literature. 3. Indians
of North America—Missions—California—Juvenile literature. 4. Indians,
Treatment of—California—History—Juvenile literature. 5. California—
History—To 1846—Juvenile literature. I. Title. II. Series.
F864.D585 2006
979.4'02—dc22   2005020411

Contents

In this painting, Indians greet Columbus as he arrives in the Americas.

Land for Spain

Spanish explorer Christopher Columbus first arrived in North America in 1492. He and his crew found a land rich in **natural resources.** They claimed the land and its riches for Spain. People already lived on the land. These people were American Indians.

nothing for the riches of the Americas. They were eager to teach the American Indians about the Catholic religion and the Bible.

For the next two and a half centuries, priests from Spain established religious communities in New Spain. These religious communities were called **missions.** The priests set up hundreds of missions in Florida, Texas, New Mexico, Arizona, and California.

The Alamo, the site where Texans fought against a Mexican army in 1836, was originally a Spanish mission.

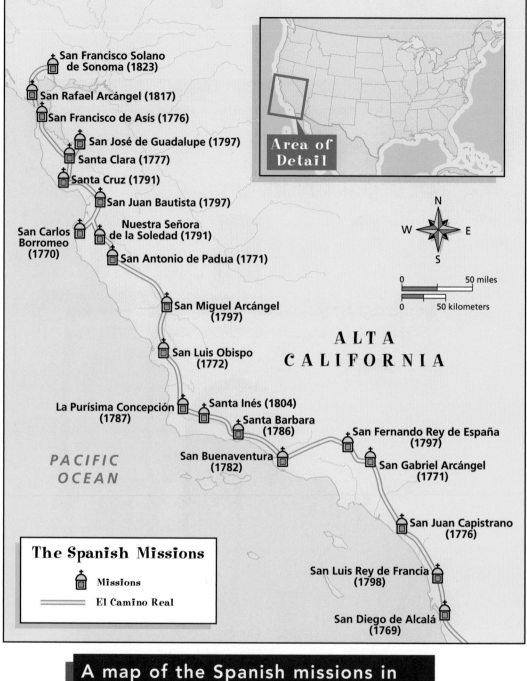

A map of the Spanish missions in California and their founding dates

Among the most famous and successful are the twenty-one missions in California. They run along the coast of California from San Diego to just north of San Francisco. The Spanish built a road to connect these missions. They used American Indians to help them with their work. This road became California's first highway. It is called El Camino Real, which is Spanish for "the king's road."

A Challenging Task

Building missions was a challenge. The priests set out with a company of soldiers. Their job was to protect the priests and the missions from Indians who didn't want to join the missions.

The Spanish sometimes traveled by land. They covered

The Spanish look for land in California to build a mission.

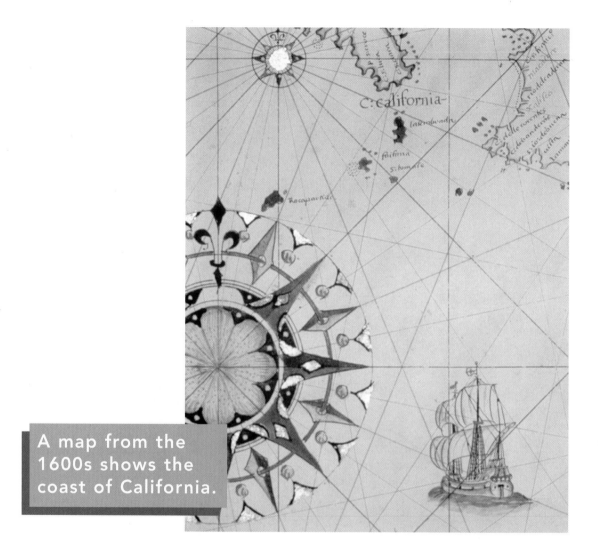

A map from the 1600s shows the coast of California.

hundreds of miles, with the priests sometimes on foot and the soldiers on horseback. At other times, they had to travel by sea. Either way, they faced harsh weather and difficult conditions.

The travelers didn't always know where they were going or what lay ahead. The maps that they used were often incorrect. The directions they had been given were often unclear. The travelers some-times ran out of food and supplies. Many died from illness along the way.

Within an area set by the Spanish government, the priests looked for land with good soil for farming and plenty of water. When they found it, they began the work of setting up a mission. Nearby, the soldiers sometimes built a military fort, or **presidio** (pronounced pray-SEE-dee-o).

Because the land had few trees, shelters could not be made of wood. The builders

Like the mission workers, people today build with adobe bricks.

used a mixture of mud and hay to make bricks called **adobe.**

Spanish priests and American Indians leave a mission chapel after a service.

For the priests, the most important building was the chapel, where religious services would be held. The priests organized kitchens, barns, workshops, classrooms, and **dormitories** to go around the chapel.

Missions were often built in a square, with a courtyard in the center and a chapel at one corner.

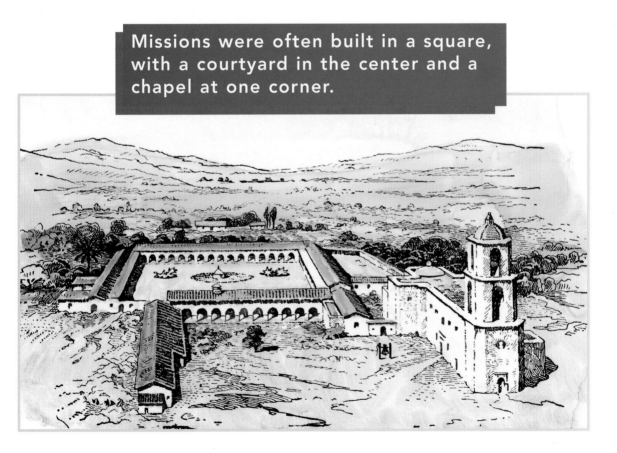

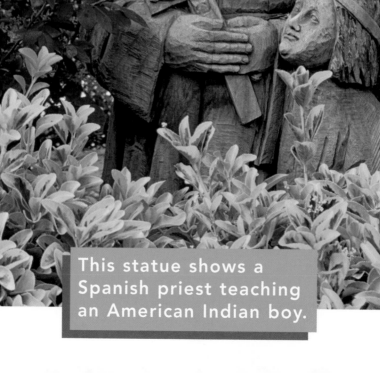

This statue shows a
Spanish priest teaching
an American Indian boy.

The priests were eager to reach out to the local Indian tribes. They wanted the American Indians to join their new community and become Christians.

Some of the American Indians were willing to accept the priests' teachings. They offered to help with the mission. Others worked for the priests in exchange for food, clothing, and other goods from Spain.

Daily Life at the Mission

Once a mission was built
and some American Indians
had joined it, the priests
set up a daily program.
Mornings began in the
chapel with a church service
called **Mass.** Breakfast was
usually a bowl of hot mush

Mass was held in the mission chapel every morning. This chapel is in Mission San Juan Capistrano.

made from corn flour. Then everyone went to work.

Each person contributed to the growth and success of the mission. The priests taught the Indians how to farm the way Europeans did. The Indians planted seeds and pulled

American Indians were part of the farming community at the missions.

Indians at the missions worked at many tasks, including crafting baskets and making rope.

weeds. Later, they picked fruits and vegetables. They had to feed the horses, cows, and chickens.

Spanish priests and American Indians used this large metal pot for cooking (top) and these stone tools for grinding corn (bottom).

At noon, the work stopped for lunch. The mission cooks served a thick soup made with meat and corn called **pozole** (pronounced po-SO-lay). For several hours each day, the priests held religious classes. The priests taught the Indians about the Catholic religion. Then everyone shared a meal of bread and corn mush.

As the sun went down, the priests went to their rooms for Bible study and prayer.

At the missions, the padres lived in small rooms with a cot, a table, and a chair.

In keeping with their beliefs, they had few possessions. There was little furniture in their rooms. The padres might have a cot or mat to sleep on, a hook to hang their robe on, a simple desk, and a wooden chair.

The Indian girls and unmarried women at the mission slept in dormitories. Married couples and their families shared small homes in a nearby village.

A Founder of California

Father Junípero Serra was born in 1713 on the Spanish island of Majorca. As a teenager, he studied to become a Franciscan priest. Serra had a great love of God and a deep desire to help others. He was an excellent student. He was also a gifted preacher.

After many years in Mexico and on the Baja California peninsula, Serra was asked to establish missions along the coast of

Father Serra

Mission San Diego de Alcalá

California. Serra founded Mission San Diego de Alcalá on July 16, 1769. It was the first mission in Alta (or Upper) California. Father Serra's work made the missions a success and opened the way for the Spanish settlement of California. The Franciscan order of priests, founded by St. Francis of Assisi in 1209, still exists.

Hardships and Heartaches

By establishing the missions, the priests believed they were helping the American Indians. They thought of the Indian people as children who needed direction and order. But the Indians were not children. They were not eager to give up their culture and customs.

American Indians gather in a mission courtyard.

Some did not want to join the priests' church.

Whether they wanted to or not, the Indians were often

forced to accept the missions and a new way of life. Many learned to adapt, but others tried to escape. Some fought to keep their land and their freedom. However, they soon discovered that it was impossible to drive out the Spanish. The military technology of the Spanish overwhelmed the Indians. In addition, thousands of Indians died from diseases that the Spanish brought with them.

Spanish explorers force American Indians to carry their loads.

The soldiers stationed at the nearby presidios could be cruel to the American Indians. They often mistreated the

Indians. The priests tried to stop the soldiers' behavior, but the local governors and Spanish rulers did not support them.

In 1821, Mexico won its independence from Spain. This meant that the missions were no longer under Spanish control. They were in Mexican territory.

The new Mexican government disliked the power of the priests. Settlers complained

Mexicans celebrate independence from Spain in 1821.

that the missions owned all the best farmland. In 1834, the Mexican government took the missions away from the priests. The government gave the missions to other leaders and landowners.

Without the devoted padres, the missions fell apart. They had been close communities with trusted leaders. Now the missions were poorly run businesses. No one took care of repairing the buildings or caring for the fields. Under these conditions, the missions could not survive for long.

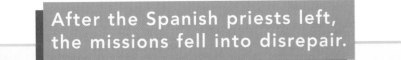
After the Spanish priests left, the missions fell into disrepair.

The Missions Today

By the 1850s, only a handful of Spanish missions were still serving their communities. Most missions had been completely deserted. The fields lay empty. Some of the buildings were no longer standing.

Over time, community groups and historical societies

Father Serra kept all his own records, some of which are on display at the museum at Mission San Diego de Alcalá.

began to realize the importance of the missions in the history of the region. People studied the letters and journals of the mission founders. Then they started to rebuild and restore the original buildings. They replanted the gardens and fields around the buildings. As historians discovered old tools, pottery, and paintings, they displayed them in the newly restored missions.

Today, the Spanish missions in Florida, Texas, New Mexico, Arizona, and California attract millions of visitors each year. Scholars, tourists, and schoolchildren come to learn what the missions have to teach about the past.

California's Mission San Juan Capistrano has beautiful buildings and gardens.

To Find Out More

Here are some additional resources to help you learn more about the Spanish missions:

 **Books**

Bial, Raymond. **Missions and Presidios.** Children's Press, 2005.

Bowler, Sarah. **Father Junípero Serra and the California Missions.** The Child's World, 2003.

Lilly, Melinda. **Spanish Missions.** Rourke Publishing, 2003.

Stein, R. Conrad. **Spanish Missionaries: Bringing Spanish Culture to the Americas.** The Child's World, 2005.

Van Steenwyk, Elizabeth. **The California Missions.** Franklin Watts, 1998.

Weber, Valerie J. **The California Missions.** Gareth Stevens, 2002.

Organizations and Online Sites

The Arizona Guide
http://www.arizonaguide.com

The Arizona Office of Tourism's official site offers an introduction to the state's cultural heritage, photographs of its Spanish missions, interactive maps, and more.

California Missions
http://missions.bgmm.com/

This site provides detailed historical, architectural, and geographical information on each of California's twenty-one missions.

California Missions Studies Association
http://www.ca-missions.org/

Check out the illustrated glossary, the photo gallery, and the useful links to related sites.

The Five Spanish Missions of San Antonio
http://www.lsjunction.com/facts/missions.htm

This site features descriptions of the five Spanish missions in the Lone Star State.

Research Starters: Spanish Missions of California
http://teacher.scholastic.com/researchtools/researchstarters/missions/

This site for teachers and students includes lesson plans, vocabulary lists, maps, and useful links.

San Antonio Missions National Historic Park
6701 San Jose Drive
San Antonio, TX 78214
210-932-1001
http://www.nps.gov/saan/

Find out about tours, exhibits, and events at the four San Antonio missions included in the National Historic Park Center.

Important Words

adobe a brick made of mud and straw

dormitories buildings with many rooms for sleeping

mainland a country's biggest piece of land, as opposed to its islands or peninsulas

Mass a Catholic church service

missions religious communities set up by people to spread their religious beliefs

natural resources things in nature that are necessary or useful to people, such as water for drinking, good soil for growing things, and forests for wood

padres Spanish priests

peninsula a piece of land that juts out into the water

pozole a thick soup made with meat and corn

presidio a Spanish military fort

Index

Meet the Author

Christin Ditchfield is an accomplished educator, author, conference speaker, and host of the internationally syndicated radio program, *Take It to Heart!* In addition to her books for parents and teachers, she has written more than forty books for children on a wide range of topics, including sports, science, history, literature, and civics. Ms. Ditchfield lives in Sarasota, Florida.